The Sinful Path to Heaven

Autobiographical Erotic Poetry

Jessica Vaughn

iUniverse, Inc.
New York Bloomington

The Sinful Path to Heaven
Autobiographical Erotic Poetry

iUniverse books may be ordered through booksellers or by contacting:

*iUniverse
1663 Liberty Drive
Bloomington, IN 47403
www.iuniverse.com
1-800-Authors (1-800-288-4677)*

*Because of the dynamic nature of the Internet, any Web addresses or
links contained in this book may have changed since publication and may
no longer be valid.*

*ISBN: 978-1-4502-2943-2 (sc)
ISBN: 978-1-4502-2944-9 (ebk)*

Library of Congress Control Number: 2010906295

Printed in the United States of America

iUniverse rev. date: 5/4/2010

Dedication

This strange collection of true life moments is dedicated
to my grandmother, Queenie.

With her eighty something years
of
heaven and hell,
she taught me how to
survive and conquer
this
wickedly sinful path to heaven.

XOXOX

Contents

Introduction

Like many writers, the written word is just another form of clay used to create art. My goal has been to create provocative and powerful art *utilizing* pornography without quite *becoming* pornography. Some may still see this collection as pornography. But then again, there are some who think the painted classic masterpieces currently housed in museums across the world are pornography.

These are completely auto-biographical sexual encounters *no matter* how unreal they may sometimes seem. So, the fireman was a fireman; the fire truck was a fire truck. The prosecutor was a prosecutor; the courthouse was a courthouse. You get the idea.

While there are many situations of role play, let the record reflect that I have never been *paid* for sex. Propositioned by men with *particular* fantasies, I have just been open minded enough to play along to fulfill those fantasies. What can I say, it was fun.

All are true *except* one: <u>Unbuttoned</u>. Although I have had *similar* encounters, I wrote this one specifically for a powerful man during our brief courtship. Sadly, he and I never actually had the chance to make this particular tryst a reality.

Chronologically first within this collection and my most sentimental is <u>Wonderland</u>. It is an encounter which touched my soul, planted passion in my body and love in my heart. I thought I captured the beauty of our innocence perfectly. Hopefully, it pulls on your memories of innocent moments fondling with *your* first love.

For those of you who know me outside of my pen name, I have a very real fear of stalkers. There *are* men who will read this book and think they can hunt me and have me. Besides, I *do* have a profession to maintain. So, I thank you in advance for keeping me safe and respecting my privacy.

To the many men captured in these poems, I have twisted emotions about my erotic life and those of you I chose to include. But to quote a very dear man recently deceased, "Don't ever regret what you did, regret what you didn't do." So on that note, I thank you for being a part of my sexual adventures and my life.

Please beware that these poems are not for the faint of heart. They are about sex. Soft sex. Innocent sex. Hard-core sex. I have listed them in categories: Easy, Moderate and Rugged. Take heed. And, I do not recommend reading this book cover to cover. No collection of poetry should be read cover to cover. Simply flip and be amazed where chance takes you.

Jessica Vaughn

The Easy Path

Afternoon Ass

Sun on the white sheets.
Lips on my neck.
Your soft goatee on my back.
Your hardness in the small of my back.

Tossed cloth falls on the carpet.

Wet fingers.
Rough explorer hands
caress my bare breasts.

Dry pressing
and
grinding.

Pinched nipples.

Moans float out the open doors.

Open legs before you.

Your eyes on
creamy flesh
creamy breasts
creamy thighs.

Fingers control me.
Your cock caresses
my

very wet lips.
Purposely teasing.

You watch the waves coming in.
Thrown pillows.
The muscles tightening.

The begging.

Enter me.
Please.

Balls slam.
Full slides.

Your eyes reveal
a
dark heart
as
quivers consume me.

Virgin tightness
traps.
Every inch.
Every pump.
Every drop.

XOXOX

Baby Doll

You're playing again.
Playing with your favorite toy.

Hard and soft.
Wet and dry.

Making me
scream
moan
beg
and
howl.

I am your baby doll.

Sitting oh so pretty on your face,
no satin no silk no lace.

Pulling my bottom down deeper.
Licking biting sucking faster.
My creamy flesh quivers
as
golden little girl curls flip in waves.

New game.

It is time.
Finally time.
Oh thank God.

It's finally fucking time.

Your cock slides teasingly
along
my lips from behind.

Big hands hard on my bottom.
Your cock slides so slowly.
Slides so tightly into my cum.

The air is full of Chance.

Pinned down
and
face down.

Your legs outside mine.
Your arms outstretched over mine.
Our fingers tightly intertwined.

Gingerly nuzzling though
my golden little girl curls.

You make love to me.

For I am your favorite play thing.
This one of a kind baby doll without a ring.

XOXOX

Drummer Boy

a one
and
a two

Are you ready for me to blow you?

Tick tock up your cock.
Tick tock it's like a rock.

Around and around and around I go.
Sucking your cock ever so slow.

Tick tock our eyes lock.
Tick tock oh holy fuck.
Sliding high and low to and fro.
You slowly melt my lost little soul.

Lips and hands and spit and cum.
Sliding licking sucking.
Oh yum.

One two.
Hands in goo.

Slide and swirl
and
watch you curl.

Shoot hard and swallow it all.

Take it all and watch you fall.

One two.

One two?

Oh, Drummer Boy.
You *had* me,
heart and all.

XOXOX

Five Star

Pristine white sheets
and
creamy naked flesh.

Soft lips caress
your
bedtime cheeks.

Rough hands
slowly explore
my thighs.
My curves.
My neck.

So slow.
So delicate.
So soft.

Time has frozen
and
the whole world
has
disappeared.

Deeply consumed.

Your hands caress my inner thighs.

My damp skin

sparkles
in the moonlight.

A porcelain greek goddess above you.

Peacefully deep.
Almost motionless.

Soft moans
and
soft whispers
float past these lips
into
warm air.

Your eyes consume
my curves.
My grace.
My beauty.

My spirit glows
as
you softly kiss
my soul.

My hair
caresses
my back.

My hands
caress
my breasts.

Deeply touched.
Deeply kissed.
Deeply in love.

Oh.

So slowly.
So gracefully.
So deeply.

Moving inside
of me.

With a few deep breaths,

I
feel
you cum
into
my soul.

XOXOX

Hooah

Florescent lit barracks halls.
Men in BDU's stare.
Mosquito wings to bars.
All strong deep stares
at me.
Walking hand in hand
with
the cowboy boots and rodeo hat
towering over me.

Southern hospitality in your small room.
Country music fills the amber lit air
behind
your locked barracks bedroom door.

That Texan accent.
No words.

Just that accent
slowly slipping under my clothes.

You lock my eyes to yours
refusing to let go.

Towering over me
the industrial bed springs creak.
Our eyes lock.

Into my wetness you politely penetrate.

Gasping deep.
Pushing deep.
Staring deep.

That deep accent
and
your deep blue eyes
deeply penetrate me.

Your rough hands caress me.
My long hair.
My pretty face.
My soft skin.

You move so soft and deep.
You stare as
intense quivers consume me.

I cum
and I cum
and I cum
putting this soldier's cock on lock down.

Tenderly.
Lips on lips.
Rough hands on my face.

Cum baby cum.

Intense blue eyes staring into me.
You press deeply into me.

So slowly into me.

Cum baby cum.

So very vulnerable.
My sweet country boy.

Cum baby cum.

Locking your glistening tan muscles
and
locking yourself so very deep into me.

You lock into my eyes.

Cumming.

Just as I ordered you to.

Hooah!

XOXOX

It Took Awhile

Four tropical drinks.
A pomegranate martini.
A margarita.
A game of pool
and
three very long years.

Teary eyes search yours.
Sweet lips kiss yours.
And suddenly.
Once again.
I'm wishing to be yours.

Let's go get naked.

Ok.

Deep swirling bubbles
cover
the body,
the man,
the *life* I missed.

You watch.
You wait.
You so badly want me.

So,
I tease you.

Sandal by sandal.
Piece by piece.
Almost naked.
Almost yours.

Watching my backside.
Hips twisting.
Thumbs down my waist
slowly peeling
my red heart covered panties.
Slowly uncovering
my heart shaped ass.

Bent before you.
Ready for you.
Now crawling to you.

Warm rich bubbles
slowly
consume
my
creamy white skin.

Kisses so wet so hard so soft.
Fingers thrust so deep up me.
Fingers dig hard through your hair.

Oh God,
how I missed this.

Thrusting in.

Sliding out.
Swirling around my clit.
Thrusting in.
Sliding out.

Moaning.
Oh, God.
Moaning.
More.
More.
More.

Cupping.
Sucking.
Biting.

Oh, God.
You're so hard.
More.
More.
More!

Grabbing.
Giggling.

Your head falls back.
Slow soapy stroking.
Little waves start to lap.

I want it.
(again)
I want to feel you inside me.

(again)
I want to feel you cum inside me.
(again)

Lowering.
Pushing.
Deeply pushing.
Yes.
Yes.
Now you're inside me.

Pumping fast.
Pinching hard.

Our bubble covered hands
together tightly lace.
Bubble covered breasts
grace your face.

Pumping.
Thrusting.
Cumming.
Oh, God.

Waves of bubbles crash on the hotel floor.

Pumping.
Thrusting.
Cumming once more.

Oh, it took a long long while.

A stripped bed.
Tossed pillows.

Our
bubble covered
steaming
naked
bodies
tightly melt together.

Oh, God.

Maybe.
Just maybe.
This will take awhile.

XOXOX

Lust

Ever crave the crave?

The kiss that erases
every
little
thing
but
flesh.

Thoughts
about
work
kids
makeup
just evaporate
into nothing
but
a soft moan.

Not caring who may see.
(Oh, I hope they see.)
The naked breast in the shadow.

Maybe even hear.
(Oh, I hope they hear.)
The soft moans through the air.

Hands groping
clothes falling

lips searching
legs spreading.

Soft flesh pressed
against
the cold floor
the cold wall
the cold sheets.

Grinding hips
moaning lips.

Longing
for this to never end.

Ever crave?

The bliss,
the lust…

of us?

XOXOX

The Secret Garden of Sin

With your hand just above my knee
you sleep like a statue beside me.

Naked except for the soft light of the moon.

I touch my cool skin
and
quietly begin to swoon.

Hard nipples.
Soft full breasts.

Such softness leading to my wet secret garden.

My breath goes deep
as my hips slowly beat.
It is your flesh I now seek.

Yet lying there wide awake,
you pretend to sleep.
Hand statuesque on my smooth thigh.

Eyes open?
Watching?

Arched back into gasping darkness.
I do not know what you see.

Touching
myself
slow,
high and low.

A deliberate intensity quivers through me.

I want you to touch me.
Restrain me.
Fuck me.

Hmmmmm.

Do you feel me cum?

As my hand glides over yours.
Over and over
again
caressing the hand of the sleeping statue.

I know you really want to.

Breaking the hold.
Breaking the spell.

I take your hand
and
twist it tight with mine.

Rising up.
You press your body hard against mine.

Lips to open lips.
Hot and hard.
Melting into me.

Hand in hand we enter my secret garden.
The forbidden wet land.

Cumming.

My perfect statue
plants his seed
deeply
into
my sinful sand.

XOXOX

Soft & Creamy

Sunkissed glistening flesh.
Wet lips.
Cum dripping.
Soft creamy skin.

Your hard cock pushes
past
my soft full red lips.

Tongue swirls.
Breasts swallow fully.

Wet.
Oh, so wet.

Tight hands on your cock.
On your balls.

Fuck my wet cleavage.

Lips kiss.
Tongue swirls.
All around your cock.

My eyes lock yours
as
your hot cum covers me.

You sink

completely satisfied
into
my deep red sheets.

XOXOX

Sparks Fly

Sparks fly.
Embers crackle.
Your tender hands move
the damp hair from my dimple.

Deeply penetrating my eyes.
So slowly.
Bare wood on my bare back.

Sparks fly as you fuck me bareback.

Shadows whisper
into
the golden darkness.

Moans.
Breathy moans.

Intensely quivering under your soft touch.
Slowly in and out under the golden glow.

Soft fingers on your cheek.
Your lips.
Your hair.

You suck gingerly
as
my long golden hair floats freely in the air.

Rough hands softly touch my breasts.
Slowly lower to just skin.
And lower tenderly hovering.
Awestruck and locked into my big brown eyes.

We're playing with fire, you know.

Sparks fly as you press hard against my thighs. We just
might.
We just might.
Ignite a fire of life tonight.

Deep inside my warmth.
Deep inside my soul.
Deliberately.
Fucking deliberately.
Golden flesh rocks in gentle waves
as sparks fly.

With a single sigh in my eyes,
you're cumming deep.

Deep.

Deeply I pull your cum.
Locking it deep inside.

Glowing with gentle tenderness.
We melt into each other
as
the
sparks

fly.

Embers crackle.
Your tender hands move the damp hair
from my dimple.

XOXOX

Unbuttoned

Your five o'clock shadow
brushes
against my cheek.

One button.
Two button.
Three.

My silk blouse
falls
to the floor.

Long hair
caresses
my arched back.

Your lips on my neck.

Manly hands in my hair.
On my black lace breast.

Your pants
lock
your feet together
on the floor.

Painted nails
on
your bare ass

pull your cock
to
my pink silky lips.

My soft creamy body.
My long blonde hair.
Gracefully
displayed
on
the dining room table
before you.

Tangled toes
in
your loose tie.

With your hands softly
on
my smooth thighs,
you
so slowly.
So carefully.
So very,
very desperately.

Enter me.

Full of flesh.
Full of you.
Full of love.

You tenderly adore

my naked body
under
the pure
pristine
light
of
sunset.

XOXOX

Wonderland

One
sunny
summer
afternoon
in the bottom bunk
with
my sweaty varsity hunk.

You'll be a man soon.

Oh so nervously our hands explore
and
one by one
our high school colors
fall
silently to the floor.

New undiscovered young flesh.
Soft and hard tan glowing flesh.
Sweaty after practice musky flesh.

All I feel.
All I hear.
All I smell.
All I *know* is you.

Passion.

Such a beautiful unexpected wonderland.

My body is passionately out of my control.

Quivering
and
panting
and
moaning.

Whispers.
Hot breath.
Shaky breath.

Whispering sweet nothings.
Weak animalistic somethings.

Falling between my craving thighs.

Quivering.
Shaking.
Creamy thighs.

Naked young flesh
welcomes you
to
the elusive treasure door.

Rocking and knocking.
You're gently begging for me to let you.

I grind my hips into you.
With you.

Soft wonderland wimpers
float
through the summer sunshine.

With your cock pressed hard
against
my young wet clit.

Your sweaty scent lures me
and
I so badly want it.

My feet press high into the top bunk.

And yes.
I think I will.
I think I will finally have
my
sweaty varsity hunk.

Whispers.
Apprehensive.
Begging hot whispers.

Caressing your sweaty chest,
your dirty baby face,
your baby soft hair.

Running my nails down
to your ass and digging deep.

My soft lips softly kiss.

Softly moan
and softly whisper.

Yes.

Yes?

Yes.

The door slowly opens
as you gingerly cross the threshold
to the treasure.
To the elusive treasure of wonderland.

And
with a few blinks
of
your beautiful blue eyes.

A few intense quivering slides.
A few strong pumps of cum.

Finally.
Finally now.
Completely content,
a *man* falls weakly into my arms
that sunny summer afternoon.

XOXOX

The Moderate Path

Choose

One night of sexual bliss
or
a lifetime of happiness.

Choose.

Black hooker eyes
and
lace covered thighs.

Or.

Middle of the night cries
and
kissing boo boos goodbye.

You say please
and in a few moments
I'm on my knees.
Seducing you.

I *am* yours.

All you want.
Anything you want.

For one night.
Only.
One night.

Slutty strappy sexy me.
All yours.

Momentarily.

Sloppy slimey slutty me.
All yours.

Til just about ten thirty.

Kissing.
Licking.
Sucking.
Slowly fucking.

One night.
Only.
One night.

But *now*.
You're all sucked out.
I'm all fucked out.
Your time is *now* out.

And while your kisses touched me
and
your love touched me,
your heart will forever be haunted by my voice.

Because,
you, my dear,

made the wrong fucking choice.

XOXOX

Erotic Angel

Naked.
I gaze down.
Hypnotized.
Like an erotic angel in the clouds.

Can anyone see me?

Downtown city lights
sparkle
like diamonds in the snow.
Traffic in tiny rows of pretty lights.

High above in the darkened hotel suite,
this erotic angel wonders.

Your big arms wrap around me.
Your roughness pushes my hair away
and
exposes my neck.

Hot breath.
Hot whispers.
Hot hands.

Move so slowly
so softly
up to my full breasts.

My eyes close and I feel you.

Naked.
I feel you.

Moving into you.
Moving on you.
Grinding my full body.

Naked.
So naked.

Squeezing my nipples.

I push your hands down.
Down.
Down into my dripping wet pussy.

My back arches.
My hand presses on the glass.
The floor to ceiling window.

My moans echo through the empty room
and
softly enter the hallway.

Groans.

You push my shoulder down.
My other hand slaps onto the glass.

The tip of your hard cock
kisses my pussy lips.

My breath steamy on the skyrise window.

Hips grind.
Pushing back.
Begging for you.

I beg.
My breath hot.
Heavy.
Panting and pleading.

I beg.

Naked.
Above the watching diamonds
of the city.

Hands firmly on my hips.
With one swift thrust,
you enter me.
Pushing me closer to the glass.

I gasp.

Oh, it's heaven.
Just like heaven.

Fucking me fast.
I grind.
Meeting your deep hard thrusts.

My nipples kiss the cool glass.

You slap my ass.
Hard.

Your hands climb high
pushing against the glass wall.

The naked erotic angel
shows herself
to the city.

Cumming.
Beautifully cumming.
Sweetly cumming
for the watching diamonds oh so pretty.

Biting my neck.
Pushing deep.
Your big hands on my tits
tightly squeezed against the glass.
Biting hard.

There is silence.
Still silence.

Naked.
I gaze down.
Hypnotized.
Like an erotic angel in the clouds.

Can anyone see me?

XOXOX

Fireguys are Sleeping

Yellow industrial stars
illuminate the shadows
as I drive.

Wind through my blonde hair.
Topless convertible in the black night.
Minimal coverage.
Midnight dew on my mocha skin.

Grill in the gravel yard.
Dispatch garble in the air.
Your body towers over mine
even with my high summer heels.

Long blonde hair kisses my bare back.

Arms engulf me.
Holding me prisoner.

Fingers explore
my
soft spaghetti strapped skin.

Reaching melting point for me.
You prepare to combat the flames.
Impressive forces stand ready.
Oh, so ready to be dispatched.

Your fingers.
Your mouth.
Your equipment.
Your cock.

All desperately needed
to
combat the out of control
passion fire
in
my body.

Your hot whispers hush my screams.

Summer skirt
busted through
to fight the raging fire.

Fire truck red painted steel
presses against my bare ass.
My heels on the steel step.

You stand between my knees.
Fully dressed.
Assessing the fire.

Taunting it.
Playing with it.

Soft silk gathered about my hips.
Your fingers clear

my sunkissed shoulders
and
breasts
of
fabric debris.

(dispatch… ignored… another house…)

More fabric falls about my hips.

Black heeled sandals.
Bare mocha summer legs.
Messy blonde hair kisses my face.

The heat glowing before you.
My hands gripping steel bars high above.

Equipment ready.

You attack.
Hands everywhere patting out the fire.
My breasts.
My ass.
My mouth.

You press your impressive body to mine.
Into the core of the passion fire
so violently fighting the fire.

I *long* to scream.

Shhh.

Fireguys are sleeping.

Oh.
I long to *scream.*

Shhh.

You pump
and
you pump
fighting this wicked wild fire
under my
glistening moonlit summer skin.

You slide against me.
In and out.
In and out of me.

Holding my breath.
Fighting to scream as you fight the fire.
My moans escape like poofs of black smoke.

Shhh.
Fireguys are sleeping.

Rocking.
Grinding.
My body is pinned.
The fire is contained.
Locked onto bars.

My body is at your mercy to save.

Sweaty.
Dehydrated.
Tired.
Determined.

You attack the core one final time.

Slow and deep.
Using your hands to aid the attack.

Your forcefully suck and squeeze my tits.
Wet lips on my ear.
Hot steam on my neck.
Cock deep and so fucking slow.

Your big hands on my inner thighs.
My legs hike up.
I am pinned to fire truck bars.

My body rocks.
Rumbles.
Rolls in waves.

Black smoke moans float out.

Shhh.
Fireguys are sleeping.

My soft
so very soft
body

locks solid
pinning your cock inside my tight pussy.

Aggressively.
You pump me
pin me
penetrate me.

Out then in.
Out then in.
Over and over again.
Out then in.
Out then in.

Grinding and grunting.

Oh.

With my fire finally out
you pull out.

Draining your big hose
all over my mocha summer thighs.

XOXOX

Mermaids

Waves crash in the distance.
Tent canvas billows.

I'm wide awake dreaming
as
she sleeps like an angel beside me.

Painted fingertips touch her.
Pouty lips caress her.
Cool nakedness presses into her.

Moonlight vision.

Soft porcelain blue curves.
More curves.

Long blonde hair.
Long brunette hair.

Quietly intertwine.
Seaside.

XOXOX

The Mirror

Strong spirits sucked down.
Denim pulled down.
On my knees I got down.
You watch me suck your cock down
in the mirror at the end of the hallway.

So hungry.
So thirsty.
Nails dig into your bare ass.

Clothes get thrown down.
On my hands I get down.
On your knees you get down.

Our eyes meet
in the mirror at the end of the hallway.

You ram you cock deep
into
my dripping wet pussy.

Wet slaps
loud slaps
off the hardwood floors.

Screams echo
grunts echo
off the long white walls.

Long hair flips back
seizing some you yank it back.
Flashing my bare soft breasts
in the mirror at the end of the hallway.

Harder we fuck.
Faster we fuck.
Louder we fuck.

Sweaty naked bodies fuck hard
in the mirror at the end of the hallway

My cunt clamps your cock down.

Oh yes.
I'm cumming.
Cumming so fucking hard.

Growling.
Grunting.
Groaning.
Hands dug so deep in my hips.

I watch you cum
in the mirror at the end of the hallway

XOXOX

Moans in the Distance

Windows down.
Wind blown hair.
Goose bumps.
Hard cold nipples.

Endless fog.
Dark corn stalk shadows.

My fingers
pull
your belt.
Your zipper.

With lipstick on your fly.

My creamy cheek presses
against
the steering wheel.

Pulling over along an endless dark road.
Just along the dark tree line
and
corn stalk shadows.

Skirt hiked over my heart shaped ass.
Panties pulled to the side.
Gripped hips in hard grinding waves.

Long hair flips back brushing your chest.

Just shadows of animals fucking.

Tighter.
Closer.
Deeper.

The moans the groans the screams the howls.

All
just
disappear
as animals fuck
in the cool dark Indiana country.

XOXOX

Mustang Lady

You drive to nowhere.
To our only somewhere.

Escaped time.

Your hand caresses soft skin
up
to my beachy jean shorts.

Then a little farther.
A little higher.

You just drive.

Soft summer blows through my long hair.

My fingers ride
the warm summer waves
out the window.
Headlights flicker from the semis.

Coming and oncoming.
In the mirrors.
Off the battered chrome.

No words.
Just blue eyes lit by reflected semi headlights.

Dare me.

Go ahead, baby.
Dare me.

Unbutton.
Unzip.

Licking my lips.
Sinking down.
My hands slowly.
Teasingly.
Provocatively.
Slide down.

Down.
Down
my beachy jean shorts.

You watch.
Lustfully moaning
as I dip into my slick wetness.

On you drive.

My hand slides up my shirt.
Tits and nipples peaking out for all to see. Flicking my
slick clit.
Just for me.

Sinking deeper into the bucket seat I slide.
Brown eyes close so slowly.
Moaning so softly.

I know how to drive this ride.

The highway wind caresses
my glowing summer skin.
Perfect pouting lips.
Wet fingers.
Hard nipples.
Peaking pussy.

All for you to see.

On you drive.
Watching.
Lustfully moaning.

Bare feet press into the black dash board.
Your unfulfilled
unquenched
lustful moaning
drives me.

Oh yes.
So close.
Slicked and flicked.
So fucking close now.

Warm wind drowns out
my
solo screams
as
the world watches
this

mustang lady.

Cumming
and
oncumming
in warm summer waves.

On you drive.
Still.
Forever lustful.

We had escaped
if only for a moment.

Alone.
Frozen time.
Frozen society.
No consequences.
No responsibility.
No fiancés.

Simply love untamed.

Highway cruising
one perfect summer night
in
that old white mustang.

XOXOX

My Velveteen Rabbit

Fingers soft across my cool bare skin.
Wet squeezed nipples.
Discover my thighs.
Just a whisper touch.

A soft buzz brushes past my breast.
Slowly down
down
down
to
wetness.

Sliding teasingly.
Playfully.

Curves squirm.

Lips part.

I am so wet.
Desperate hips
thrust
to welcome heaven.

Twisting deep.

Bunny ears buzzing

so
intensely
backwards.

Leaving my clit neglected.

With
my thighs tight
my wet fingers move quick.

Panting.
Thrusting.
Grinding.

I slide the control for even more.

And
pinch my cool hard nipples some more.

As
loud moans float out the window.

As
my creamy naked flesh quivers in silence.

I cum.

XOXOX

My Waterfront Trysts

Parked cars.
Picnic blanket.
Picturesque stroll.

To the water.
To the shore.
To the spot where we always fuck.

Laying you in the shade.
Tasting you.
Teasing you.
Taunting you.

Rising you like the rushing water.
Hard.

Fishermen calls echo off the sand
and
through the trees.
As my panties join the leaves.

I stand over you.
Your big hands caress my thighs
dipping into my wetness.

My knees get weak.
I fall as

your cock slides in so deep.

Swaying.
Trees in the wind.
My body with your bends.

Lifting.
Long.
Lingering thrusts.

Squeezed nipples through my soft silk shirt.

Rip tide takes me.
Wave after wave.
Cumming.
The princess ship rides the waves.
Wave after quivering wave.

Then.

Looking up to you.
Red wet lips on you.
Tasting my cum on you.

Rushing water echos off the cliff.
Standing strong as the oaks around us,
you quietly gasp.

And,
with a few strong pumps
I deeply swallow
every

sweet drop
of
our cum.

XOXOX

Sexy & Wet

Take my hand
and
lead me from the sand.

Under shady trees
on my knees.

Slow and deep.
My eyes search yours.

Hmm.

Lips open.
Glistening.

Now.

Tree bark pushes hard
into my shoulder.

Wet.
Sweaty.
Hot breath
on my breast.
on my neck.

Creamy wetness exposed
discovered
deeply penetrated.

Bark digs into my back
as
your cock rams my cunt.

Hot.
Sweaty.
Panting.

Tree limbs
and
naked flesh
sway.

Moving in creamy waves.

Your mouth
catches a nipple
under
the flickers of sunlight.

With
claw marks on your ass.
My raw back shoved into the bark.
Bite marks on my neck.
Hard flexed arms grip the bark.

So still.
We're so still
under the flickering sunlight.

Waves of ecstasy.

Quivers of delight.

Splashes.
Laughter.
deafening silence.

Head thrown back.
Mouth wide open.

Only your cock ejaculating inside me
and
our hearts beating with intense harmony.

Motionless.

You roar.

XOXOX

Seaside Shower

Sand.
And more sand.
Fucking sand everywhere.

Saltwater quickly drying
on
our sunburned skin.

Smiling and giggling.

Speed racing you
to
the outdoor beach shower.

There *is* a door.

Quickly stripping naked
dumping out sand onto our bare feet.

The clean water runs
oh so cool
down my sunset lit body.

Soap discovered.
Your hands caress and clean.
Didn't know my breasts were that dirty.

Soap stolen.
My hands discover you.

So hard.

So very swollen.

More soap
and more soap
scrubbing you hard.

Little hands tight on your hardness.
Stroking.
Soap glides soft on your tight balls.
Smoothly caressing.

Your big hands squeeze my nipples.

Touching.
Rubbing.
Fondling.
My soapy softness.

Your body falls into the wooden shower wall.

Weak knees.
Lost balance.

Soon now.
Soon now.
You will cum.

Slippery soapy hands tightly pump.

Hard.

Fast.

Soon now.
You will cum.
Eyes close.
Arms fall.

Soon now.

Soapy
full
hard
tight pumps.

So soon now.

Arms slamming the walls.
Eyes searching the sunset sky.
You groan.
Covering my hands with your cum.

Slow final strokes
of your soapy cum covered cock.

Then, a dying groan.
Swallowed into the silent water.

Rushing.
Crashing.
Splashing water.

XOXOX

Strappy Black Lacy Things

Keep your glasses on, baby.
You're gonna want to see this.

As my hand caresses your face.
Your cheek.
Your hair.
My lips softly touch your lips.

My long hair gently falls into your face
as your hand finally discovers
my hip covered in black lace.

Hands move slowly
from
black sheer covered feet
to
high thigh bare flesh.

Black straps
and
begging wetness.

Then
a layer of black lace
tight across my heart shaped ass.

Hips curve in and more bare creamy flesh.

Your fingers play me.
Play a symphony on my soul.

Your eyes
on
my glowing body.

Slowly rocking with your orders.
Controlling my waves of cum.

Hot breath on my thigh
as
you intently watch
the waves come in.

The tightly black lace wrapped waves.

Our feet intertwine.
Our legs caress.
Your hands explore.

Black lace wrapped hips.
Black strapped ass.

Slide into me, baby.

Grinding into you.
Beckoning you.
Demanding you.
Begging you.

Slide into me, baby.

Outstretched hands
dig into the headboard.
Black dipped legs tightly crossed.

Kiss my soul, baby.

Your hand
on
the small of my back
as
you slide
in and out
of
my pretty pink wet pussy.

Strapped hips.
Strapped ass.

Your heaven.
Your way.
Your control.

So tight.
So wet.
So slutty.
So fucking hot.

Finally releasing your cum.
Your shackles.
Your *soul.*

With
burning stares
into
my strappy black lacy things.

Oh, baby.
Aren't you glad you kept your glasses on.

XOXOX

The Rugged Path

Beauty and the Beast

Your eyes tell all upon our first meet.
Just another hungry beast hunting fresh meat.

You kiss me sweetly and call me beautiful.

But under the suit.
Under the smile.

I see the fangs you have tried to hide.
Weakly trying to appear innocent.

I see your wild side.

Tempting.
Alluring.
Dangerous fangs.

But I'm in heat
and I'm begging.
Please fuck me deep.

Call me bitch.
Call me whore.
I'm the one who invited you
through my door.

Shove your fingers up my cunt.

Your wedding finger up my ass.

Ask if I like that.
Ask who do I love.

I'm such a naughty girl
and
I've been so bad.

Shove into me and spank me red.

It's your pussy.
Your ass.
Yes,
I am your perfect little mistress.

Thick tongue on my face my eyes tight shut.
Call you daddy as your hot breath growls slut.

Hands pulse tight on my neck.

My so very soft shallow cries grow silent.

Silent.
Shaking.
Seizures of orgasm.
As you pump me full of cum.

Fangs retract and the beast falls.

My creamy wet beauty drips with our cum
and

at least I now know what I have become.

XOXOX

The CEO's New Toy

His time.
His money.
His power.

Using every bit of it,
he has definitely earned it.

I
am
the CEO's new toy.

I kiss him.
I tie him.
I slap him.

And.

I call him Bitch Boy.

Get on your knees,
Bitch Boy.

Slap.

Suck harder,
Bitch Boy.

Slap.

I fucking said harder,
Bitch Boy.

What a bad bad new toy
calling the CEO Bitch Boy.

Fuck me,
Bitch Boy.

Slap.

Fucking harder,
Bitch Boy.

Slap.

Fuckin do it,
Bitch Boy.

I slap him.
I fuck him.
I choke him.

Now cum,
Bitch Boy.

Slap.

Fucking do it,
Bitch Boy.

Choke.

Now!
Bitch Boy!

Using every bit of it,
he has definitely earned it.

This naked cum covered toy
who calls the CEO Bitch Boy.

XOXOX

Four Martinis

Pomegranate martinis.
Bar blinds open.

Afternoon sun lights up your face.

Your eyes on my lips.
On my
black silk covered
oh
so full breasts.

Purposely
brushing up hard
against
your arm every time I turn.

'projected outcome'
'itinerary'
'stage one'
'stage two'
'agendas'

Such a professional discussion
of
our sex plans.

Our afternoon tryst.

Professionally outlining

our
sex play
for
all to hear.

But no one was the wiser.

Your cologne drifts to me
as
I whisper in your ear.

Your hard cock
mostly hidden
by
your suit jacket.

Money thrown
to
the bartender.

Stage 1

My door opens.
My door closes.

Your eyes search mine.
Sweet shy kisses.

One button.
Two button.
One buckle.
One clasp.

One zipper.

Your hands caress
my curvy hips
as
I bend over to remove
my
high black boots.

One zipper.
One clasp.

Flesh.
All flesh.
Cool wet flesh.

Sub-Stage 2 of Stage 1

My naked breasts
press
against your knees.

My eyes look up into yours
begging please.

My lips
softly touch
slowly
underneath.

My breath deep.

Base to the tip.
Head tilted full back.
Mouth open.
Base to tip.
Slowly loving all of it.
Base to tip.

Sub-Stage 3 of Stage 1

Your turn.

You kiss me
pushing me on my back.

Hand on my inner thigh.
Pressing.
Opening.
My body quivers as my hands fly high.

As all muscles contract
over and over again.

Lips so soft.
Fingers so deep.

Panting.

Hands digging on carpet.
.
Your body
moves softly
against mine

until
our lips meet.

Moans.
Quivers.

Your cock
kisses
my
silky
cum dripping
lips
and
slowly
so
slowly
slides right in.

You enter
and
enter some more.

Oh.

So fucking deep.

Rocking.
Grinding.

Hands slam
the
hallway walls.

Pure hot passion.

Sub-Stage 4 of Stage 1

I slide my body up.

Tits in your face.
Lips on your ears.

Cooing.
Moaning.

You feel so fucking good.

Hips open.
Pressing firm.
Pressing deep.

Grinding.

Hands
softly
guide
my hips.

gonna cum gonna cum gonna cum

As my head flys back.

No moans.
No breath.

No screams.

Silence.
Pure silence.

As
you
pump
me
full of cum.

Stage One Complete.

XOXOX

Heaven or Hell

In the hip grinding inferno,
there are only four men who *know*.

With the band playing hard core punk,
it is these four who *know*
the feel of my cunt.

One I tenderly kiss goodbye at his car
while I leave another all alone at the bar.
Then I smack one on the ass as I leave
going home with the man most in need.

Naked.
I wait.

In the dark.
On his bed.
Under the fan.

It's heaven.
Pure heaven.

Soft kisses
and
slow hands.

Please
forget baby.
Forget.

Ignore heaven ignore hell.
This just might be all you're meant to get.

Spooning me.
Slowly sliding into me.
Simply making love to me.

Pumping deeper.
Kissing deeper.

Oh, forget baby.
Forget.

Grinding into him.
Closer.
Closer now.
Deeper into him.

Strong arms wrap around me.
Pinching and squeezing so tenderly.
Soft fingers on his balls below me.
Caressing and rolling so so softly.

Yes, baby.
Forget, baby.

Just
like
that
baby.

Oh.

Moaning and arching.
I cum.

Pumping.
Pulling.
Grinding.
Grunting.
He cums.

Oh, forget baby.
Forget.
Ignore heaven ignore hell
because maybe this is all you get.

In the dark.
In my arms.
In the *screaming* silence.

His tears fall.

Kissing skin.
Kissing tears.

Holding him softer.
Holding me harder.

He lays in my arms silently crying
for his best friend who is slowly dying.

And while I kiss away his many tears,
I am overflowing with a growing fear.

While tonight I am doing what I can,
I am deeply in love with another man.

So, please.
Please.
Do tell.

Will I be going
to heaven?

Or to hell.

XOXOX

In a Van Down by the River

My eyes.
My lips.
And,
my spread legs
say
take me as you wish.
I am yours.

Your hands move up my thigh.
My long black skirt piles around my hips.

Hot breath
on
my neck.
My lips.
Bare breasts.

You suck so hard.
Hands grope so hard.

Groping.
My hair.
My shoulders.
My ass.

Your hands push hard
past fabric

until there is nothing
but
bare
white
sacrificial flesh.

Sounds of rushing water
creep
though the blinds
as
our steamy sweaty bodies
move about
in the dark shadows.

Red lips surround you.
Deeper and deeper.
Slowly swirling your cock
with my tongue.
Again and again and again.

Rough big hands in my hair.
Pushing and pulling.
Control me.
All yours.
In and out.
Deeper faster my lips move.

My fingers caress your balls.
You search my wet pussy.
My tits.
Not enough hands.
Desperately need

more hands
all over my naked body.

Pushing up and down.
Deeper and faster.

Pumping my red lips with your cock.

Panting.
Groaning.

Your sweaty muscles
glisten
in the slivers of sunlight.

Up on my knees.

You stroke your wet
oh so hard
cock.

Pushing my tits together.
Licking my lips.
Tasting.
Mouth open.

Oh, please?

You whisper.

Are you my whore?

Watching your eyes for lust.
Watching your cock for cum.
Swollen breasts heaving.

Yes.
Mmm.
Yes.
I
am
your whore.

You stroke faster
on
my tongue.
Red open lips teasing the tip of your cock.

Whenever.
Wherever.
However.

My body rocks with you.
Wet tits and lips kissing your cock.

Then.
With a deep surrounding exhale.

You cum.

Sinfully blessing
my
swollen tits
and

open red lips
with
your copious sweet cum.

Hmmm.

Yes.
Swallowing and licking my lips.
Rubbing your cum into my tits.

I am your whore.

XOXOX

Midnight at the Marina

Dense darkness.
Steamy moist skin.
Deep blue water.

Flesh comes free.
Clothes on a tree.
Water slowly consumes me.

Open arms.
Open legs.

All tightly wrap around you.

Such strength.
Such masculinity.
Such steel.

Locked passion-filled eyes search me.

I know.
I deeply know.
That in a moment…

You *will* be fucking me.

Pinning me to the concrete wall
hands hard on my tits

My back.
My ass.

You barge in without asking.

Water vanishes between us.
Soft splashes.

Quiet.
Heavy.
Breath.

Deep eyes.

No more words.
No more splashes.
No more breath.

Wet.
Deep.
Tongue filled.
Kisses.

My body locks in your arms.
Quietly cumming.

As my distracted husband
watches
the incoming shadowy waves
from afar.

XOXOX

Perfect Service

Fucking shopping.
I hate shopping.
But.
I am shopping
for a fuck.

The special shopper
guided to the back room by the manager
for the special private collection.

Pushing your linebacker shoulders
against
the tall towers of stock.
Brown batting eyes lock.

My hand squeezes your huge hard cock.

Yes.
I did.

Quick.
Quick.
Quick.
My tongue flicks your lips.

Unzip.

My warm soft hands dig so quick.
Softly touching first the tip.

Then all of it.

On my knees now I lick.

Your head flies back.
Wet swirls.
Deep swirls.
Fast swirls.

Your hands cling to the top of the towers.

Giving me what I want.
Giving me what I demand.
Giving me perfect quick service
with
silent moans and groans.

It is *you* who I now own.

Looking into your weakened eyes.
I thank you.

Then away I walk.
Licking my perfect untouched lipstick.

XOXOX

Prosecute Me

Red lips.
Glitter black eyes.
Big hair.

Secretary stares.
My short skirt.
Tiny tight top.
High heels.

A hooker with a Coach purse.

He'll be right with you.

Fake files in hand.
Past staring eyes.
There you are.

Big man guides me
down
the old echoing halls
of
the court house.

Just quietly following
the suit
the files
the man of the court house.

Quietly following you.

Bookcases line the room.
The prep room.
The interrogation room.

We lock eyes
as you
lock the door.

Diving into my cleavage.
Your hands on my ass.

You lift me
onto
the hundred year old legal table.

Suit jacket falls to the floor.
Fingers unbutton.
Your big hands reveal
my creamy flesh.

Your lips and hands
suck and squeeze my nipples.

Panting.
Fingers enter me.

Soft moans forever
get *lost* in the law books.

Legs spread before you.
Floating high heels.

My soft hands on my breasts.
Cool wood on my bare back.

You step back
and
take it in for a moment.

Staring into my hooker eyes.
Forward you press into me.

Sunlight catches your fast pumps.

Pants down.
Hands on curvy hips.
Pulling deep.
Pushing hard.

The hundred year old law table creaks.

The prosecutor fucks a hooker
in the court house.

Your fantasy.
Your desire.
Your vision.

A wet slutty pussy
for
your big man cock.

Fucking hard and fast.
Seizing sinful flesh.

Then.
Immediately.
Swift as a guillotine.

You cum.

XOXOX

The Suite

Ice clinks.
The clock blinks.
Last moment check
in the mirror above the sink.

With one hand I sip my Tandoor
and with the other hand I open the door.

Hello.

My hand reaches
into the hallway
grabbing your belt
pulling you into my suite.

Your picture doesn't do you justice.

The door closes
and
I push you onto the couch.

Lamp light glows from the bedroom.

Another long sip.
Setting it down.
I lick my lips.

Your hands run
under my long black skirt

up my soft skin
to my hips.

Black lace panties fall to the floor.

I kneel before you
sweetly smiling
looking up at you.

Unbuckle.
Unzip.

Now.
Black lacey covered breasts press into your face.

Hiked up skirt.
Hands on my bare ass.
You tightly slide into me.

We grind.
Rising and falling.

My hips.
My chest.
No words
from
my lips.

Sweetly you run your hands
through my hair.
Playing with my ears.
Playing with my clit.

Red flushed skin
above
your perfectly starched collar.

Pretty painted fingers
in
your perfect silk tie.

Lustful eyes search mine.

Forward.
Backward.
Upward.
Downward.

We fuck in perfect harmony.

Running a finger across your lips,
into your mouth.

I cum.
Cum.
Cumming all over you.

Your hands grip hard into my arched back.
So much tighter
pressing deeper and harder.

With your face in black lace.
You stop.
Stop deep.

Grunt deep.

There is a still silence.

Until finally,
you slowly grind
with
a long deep exhale.

Slipping on my panties.
Straightening my skirt.
Sipping my Tandoor.

I am sweetly satisfied.

But.
Oh, yeah.

*I'm sorry.
I forgot.*

What did you say your name was?

XOXOX

Sin

Pink roses.
Oh, how I love pink roses.

Sweet coffee.
Touching knees.
Conversation on worldly topics.
Deep eyes.
Soft skin.

My eyes
caress
your cheeks
your neck
your ears
your lips.

Then,
bar stools
cigarettes
liquor.

Your hand
on my bare thigh
softly caresses
my skin.

Risqué conversation.
Whispers in my ear.
Breath heavy in my hair

exhaling down my neck.

Sounds.
No real words.

It wasn't about the words anymore.

I whisper back
letting my lips
softly touch
your ear.

Letting my breath
softly touch
your neck.

Letting my hard nipples
softly touch
your chest
through your perfectly starched shirt.

You grab my hand walking to the car
pulling me close.
Kissing me deep.

A hard deep kiss.

Open door to the car.
Pressed against the car.

I feel you.
I feel your heat.

I feel your cock.

Eyes searching.
Lips searching.
Your body hard against mine.

Then a whisper.

Do you want to go somewhere?

Just a whisper.

Yes.

Darkness fills the room.
Light beams through the cracks
of
the hotel drapes.

I slowly sip my Tanquaray.

On your knees
between my knees.
My head falls back
as
rough hands
and
soft lips
slowly make their way
up my long skirt.

Red panties fall to the floor.

You
softly
gently
roughly
taste me
lick me
bite me.

My nails dig into the back of your head
as I cum.

Hours
of
naked
soft
hard
flesh.

Hours of Tanquaray.
Hours of lost time.

Hmmm.

While your scent still lingers on my skin.
T''is only an innocent beginning
to the final sin.

XOXOX

Welcome Home, Honey

Here you come loosening your tie.
T'is just another long day gone by.

Welcome home, honey.

Your cheeks flush
and
you suddenly soften your rush.

Staring.
Smiling.

Slowly soaking in the sheer sight of me.
Quietly laying in bed.

Black hooker eyes.
Black strap covered thighs.

Wet red lips.
Black lace covered hips.
With a single red stiletto
rocking over my knee.

Staring.
Smiling.

You come to me.

To smell me.
To taste me.
To feel me.

Fingers disappear between my thighs.

Thrusting hard.
Biting hard.
Pulling hard.

I am suddenly cumming
with
a few silent cries.

You step back.

Undressing
and
planning
your
new attack.

Welcome home, honey.

My fingers stroke your cock.
My tongue teases your cock.

Red lips take it all in
as
you caress curvy skin.
Heaving skin.

Red embroidered black bustier
pushed up skin.

Shoving fingers deep inside me.

Tongue wet upon me.
Your big hands move me.

Ass in the air.
Pulling my hair.

You ram your bare cock deep inside me.

Hands on my hips.
You pull out just to the tip.

Long and deep.

You're such a fucking slut.

Faster and faster and faster.
We fuck.

Whose whore are you?

Deeper and deeper and deeper.
We fuck.

Yours daddy all yours
all yours
your whore daddy.

Then.
Suddenly.
You're cumming
and
cumming
and
cumming
deep inside me.

Hair pulled.
Ass spanked.
Red stilettos on the floor.
At the end of every long day gone by,

I am your whore.

XOXOX